Published by Creative Education
123 South Broad Street, Mankato, Minnesota 56001
Creative Education is an imprint of The Creative Company

Designed by Stephanie Blumenthal

Photographs by Anne Gordon Images (Gillian Bailey, Anne Gordon), Archive Photos,
Richard Cummins, Image Finders (Jim Baron, Mark E. Gibson), Gunter Marx, Paul McMahon,
Bonnie Sue Rauch, Mrs. Kevin Scheibel, Karlene V. Schwartz

Library of Congress Cataloging-in-Publication Data

Shofner, Shawndra.
Apples / by Shawndra Shofner.
p. cm. — (Let's investigate)
Includes index.
ISBN 1-58341-192-5
1. Apples—Juvenile literature. [1. Apples.] I. Title. II. Let's
investigate (Mankato, Minn.)
SB363 .S54   2001
634'.11—dc21   00-047387

First edition

2 4 6 8 9 7 5 3 1

APPLES

SHAWNDRA SHOFNER

Creative Education

APPLE
ORIGIN

The first apples were probably an accident of nature, the result of two crabapple trees crossbreeding.

APPLE
REALITY

An apple tree grown from seed has one chance in a thousand of bearing fruit as good as the apple it came from.

Wildflowers share space in this apple orchard

The apple is one of our favorite fruits. People grow apples around the world because they taste good, keep well, and can be used in many ways. Apples have been an important food source throughout human history—including prehistoric times. Today, more than 7,500 kinds of apples exist. They grow on every continent except Antarctica and are marketed around the world. New varieties have been developed that stay fresh longer so that grocery stores everywhere can carry apples from halfway around the globe. It's not unusual to find apples from Japan, New Zealand, and Canada being sold next to each other.

The apple probably originated around two and a half million years ago in central and southwestern Asia. The first apples were bitter and about the size of apricots. Even so, archaeologists have found fossilized apple remains where prehistoric people used to live. These remains, from what is now Switzerland, show that people ate and used the bitter apples.

APPLE
ACCIDENT

Roman soldiers who were sent to conquer Britain unknowingly spread apple trees throughout England when the seeds from the apple cores they threw away sprouted.

APPLE
FAME

The Mutsu, a cross between the Golden Delicious and a variety of Japanese apple, is known in Japan as the "million dollar apple."

Apple trees are home to a variety of wildlife

5

When people first began using apples, they gathered them from wild apple trees. It is not clear when they learned how to grow them in **orchards**, but archaeologists have found evidence of apple trees **cultivated** by people who lived in Palestine in about 2000 B.C. In 300 B.C., Alexander the Great found cultivated apple trees in Asia Minor and brought some back to Greece. By the first century A.D., the Romans were growing about 36 different kinds of apples.

APPLE
HISTORY

One of the oldest known apple varieties still in existence today is the golden-yellow, Red-cheeked Lady apple. It was a favorite of Louis XIII of France.

*Above, the Red-cheeked Lady apple
Left, Golden Delicious is the second most popular variety*

APPLE

In England in the mid-1600s, Oliver Cromwell banned pies, including apple pies, because he believed that anything so pleasurable must be wicked.

APPLE BELIEFS

Apples have been part of religions, myths, rituals, and legends for millions of years. Many people believe that the forbidden fruit eaten by Adam and Eve in the Bible was an apple. During the Jewish holiday of Rosh Hashanah, people eat honey-dipped apple slices in hopes of ensuring a sweet new year. Haroset, a mixture of nuts, wine, spices, and apples, is part of the traditional Jewish Passover celebration.

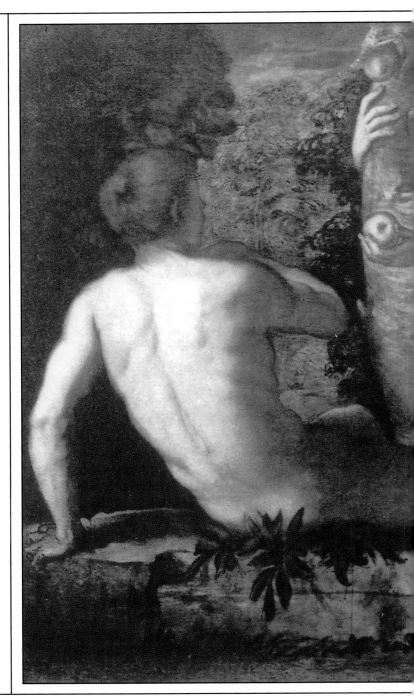

The apples in mythology are often golden and magical. In a story from Scandinavia, Idhunn kept magical golden apples and fed them to the gods in exchange for staying young. An old Irish tale tells of King Cormac mac Art, who traded his wife and children for a branch of nine golden apples that made beautiful music. From the Greeks came a myth in which Mother Earth presented the golden apple tree of eternal life to the goddess Hera on her wedding day.

Wassail (WAHS-ul) is a traditional English drink made from apple cider and ale. Wassailing began as a winter ceremony intended to bring a good **harvest***. People danced and sang around the orchard's tallest tree and tossed cups of wassail on the tree's trunk and roots.*

9

Left, one artist's portrayal of Adam and Eve Far left, an apple's skin protects its soft flesh

APPLE

PREDICTION

More than 100 years ago, British girls threw the whole peel of an apple over their shoulders and looked for their sweetheart's initials in the shape of the coiled strip.

A famous painting of William Tell and his son

Around the world, the apple and its seeds, stems, peels, and cores have been twisted, thrown, and squeezed in rituals. Romans in the first century B.C. flicked apple seeds at the ceiling. If they stuck, it meant that the person the "flicker" adored loved him in return. Celtic boys who lived more than 2,000 years ago in what is now the United Kingdom bobbed for apples to find out if the girls they liked felt the same way about them.

People have become famous because of the apple, too. Sir Isaac Newton is said to have first understood gravity when an apple fell from a tree he was sitting under. Swiss patriot William Tell refused an Austrian officer's order and was forced to shoot an arrow at an apple set on his own son's head. He succeeded, and people have been telling his story ever since. The barefoot missionary John Chapman, nicknamed Johnny Appleseed, planted apple trees as he traveled the United States.

APPLE
FACT

Bobbing for apples is a traditional children's game. Apples float because they are 25 percent air, making them lighter than water.

Above, a postage stamp honoring Johnny Appleseed

APPLE
GROWING

Of all fruit trees, apples are the easiest for the novice gardener to raise because they need little attention.

Apple tree support fences are called espaliers

At first, people planted apple seeds when they wanted to grow more trees, but they could never be sure what kind of apple they would get. That's because apple trees grown from seed won't bear fruit exactly like the apple from which the seed came. Instead, it's a mystery what kind of apples the trees will yield.

Branches from the last living tree planted by the famous Johnny Appleseed were successfully grafted onto healthy rootstock in Tennessee in August 1998.

13

S ome mystery apples were better than others. Around 400 B.C., the Greeks began to practice **grafting** to create new trees that grew the best of the mystery apples. They cut a branch or bud, known as a scion, from a good apple tree and fastened it to the **rootstock** of a tree whose apples they didn't like. The scion and the rootstock together formed a new tree that kept on producing the good apples. Today, trees are grafted in much the same way. Sometimes, though, trees do grow from seeds, and sometimes the apples they produce are good. The Granny Smith apple, for example, is said to have sprouted from apples left to rot by a Mrs. Smith in New South Wales, Australia, in 1868.

Spy apples are a juicy variety

I t can take up to six years before apple trees are ready to produce their first apples. They are ready when apple flowers bloom in the late spring or early summer. Just because a tree blooms doesn't mean it will produce apples, though. If the blossoms don't get **pollen** from the blossoms of another apple tree— with the help of insects and the wind—they won't be fertilized and won't develop into apples. That's why garden centers tell their customers to plant more than one apple tree, and it's one of the reasons trees grouped together in orchards produce more fruit.

APPLE
F A C T

The apple is a pome fruit, which means its core contains five seed chambers in the shape of a star. A fully pollinated apple will have ten seeds—two in each of its chambers.

Above, seed star
Left, a bee pollinating
an apple blossom
Far left, apple blossoms

APPLE

16

An apple tree with winter supports

THE APPLE ORCHARD

The apple orchard is a busy place throughout the year. During the winter, while apple trees are **dormant**, growers **prune** their branches. This opens the trees up to more sunlight and helps them produce apples that are big and colorful.

When spring arrives, growers clear the brush that was left from pruning. They may graft scions and plant new trees. Some growers start planning how they will control insect pests and diseases by beginning integrated pest management. They do this by watching the weather, looking for signs of disease on their trees, and hanging insect traps around the orchard to find out how many good and bad insects they have. The information they collect helps them decide if and when to spray, and how much spraying they'll need to do. Growers try not to spray too much because that can harm the trees and their fruit.

APPLE
PESTS

Aphids, apple maggots, bag worms, canker worms, codling moths, and fall webworms are some troublesome apple pests.

Above, some apple blossoms are pink Left, this Canadian orchard blooms white

APPLE

The University of Vermont Horticultural Research Center has a collection of more than 120 different kinds of crabapple trees. It is one of the largest such collections in the United States.

18

In late spring and early summer, the apple trees bloom. Most apple growers rent hives of honeybees to carry pollen from tree to tree. When small apples start to form, growers thin them so the tree will produce fewer but larger apples. They prune the tree's branches again in late summer so the ripening fruit is exposed to more sun.

Above, Malus Zuni crabapples
Right, crabapple blossoms

APPLE

CARE

Apples should be stored in a sealed plastic bag away from other fruits and vegetables because the ethylene gas they give off speeds the ripening of other fruits and vegetables.

Above, bagged apples ready to be shipped

In the fall, the apples are ready to harvest. They are picked by hand, not machine, so they won't be bruised. Then the apples are taken to a packing facility where they're washed, rinsed, graded, sorted according to size, and hand-packed into trays. Most are also **waxed**. Some are boxed and shipped to super-markets, restaurants, and schools around the world. Others are put in "controlled atmosphere storage," cold, airtight rooms where they can be kept for up to 12 months without spoiling.

KINDS OF APPLES

Apples range in size from as small as golf balls to as large as softballs. They ripen in shades of green, red, orange, and yellow. Some are eaten fresh. Some are used in salads, sauces, and pies. Others are used to make juice and **cider**.

APPLE RECIPE

The oldest apple recipe on record was found in a Roman cookbook from the third century A.D. It calls for diced pork and Matian apples.

21

Harvesting apples by hand is hard work

APPLE
DISEASES

The names of apple diseases describe what the diseases look like: apple scab, fire blight, and powdery mildew.

Above, waxed Granny Smith apples
Right, harvested Spartan apples in the orchard

Most **commercial** growers raise only apples that keep well, resist disease, and look good. Most grocery stores carry four or five fresh varieties that come from commercial growers. However, these varieties are a very small sample of the tastes and textures found in apples around the world.

A good place to find other apple varieties is at an orchard. Some grow only the kinds of apples that thrive in their region; others may grow apples of a certain color or apples that are good for pies and desserts. Still others may grow apples that were popular in the past, called "antique" or "heirloom" varieties. Some orchards even develop new varieties.

APPLE
BENEFIT

Eating a crunchy apple cleans the teeth by scraping away some of the plaque and bacteria that cause cavities.

APPLE
REFERENCE

To find out how many times an apple tree has bloomed, count the ridges left on the branch after the scales that protect the buds fall off in the spring.

This British apple orchard looks like a garden

I n the field of **pomology**, scientists and researchers work to improve the breeding of apples. Among the results of their research is the introduction of trees that yield more fruit and are more resistant to disease. In addition, scientists have assisted farmers in establishing better packing and shipping conditions so that apples are bruised less in transit. To do this, researchers developed an electronic apple—a wax apple with a computer microchip embedded inside. As the fruit is transported from orchard to grocery store, the electronic apple measures such conditions as temperature and humidity, as well as handling procedures. This information is then used to assist scientists and growers in their continuing efforts to provide consumers with a better product.

APPLE
FAMILY

Apples are members of the rose family. Some other apple relatives in this family are the pear, peach, raspberry, almond, nectarine, strawberry, and mountain ash tree.

25

Left, Empire apples are a cross between McIntosh and Red Delicious
Far left, an apple arbor

APPLE
NUTRITION

France's classic dessert apple, the Calville Blanc, has almost as much vitamin C as an orange.

APPLE
RECORD

The largest apple ever picked weighed more than three pounds (1.4 kg).

Some apple varieties are self-fruitful, making fruit with their own pollen

APPLES AND HEALTH

The apple is a nutritious food. One medium-size apple has only 80 calories, no fat, no cholesterol, and no sodium. It's a good source of potassium, fiber, and vitamins A and C. Studies have shown that including apples in a healthy diet may help fight colds, headaches, and diseases, including high blood pressure and some forms of cancer.

I t's easy for people to add apples to their diet. Apples can be baked, broiled, boiled, dried, diced, sliced, sauced, steamed, stewed, juiced, frozen, fried, or pickled. They turn up in main dishes and desserts, but most often, people simply eat them fresh.

APPLE
EQUIVALENT

If a recipe for cake or muffins calls for oil, the same amount of applesauce can be used instead to make the food lower in fat.

Above, Empire apples Left, a traditional method of cooking apple butter

APPLE
CURE

An old remedy for warts was to rub an apple half on the wart, then tie the apple back together and bury it.

APPLE
MUSEUM

The National Fruit Collection in England boasts the most complete living apple tree museum in the world. It has about 2,300 varieties.

Many farmsteads and backyards include apple trees

APPLE USES

Apples are not just for eating, though. Early medicine used apple mixtures to treat such health problems as swelling and stomachaches. An early treatment for depression called for apple juice. Distilled cider, known as applejack, was used as an **antiseptic** and an **anesthetic** for surgery.

Apples can also be decorative or useful around the house. People make wreaths from dried apple slices. They carve faces into fresh apples and then leave them to shrivel into doll heads that look like old people. A person may add an apple to a bag of potatoes to keep them from sprouting or store an apple with cookies to help them stay moist. Putting sliced apples out where something smells bad will usually clear the odor within six hours.

APPLE
PROVERB

An old saying goes, "An apple a day keeps the doctor away," because apples have long been considered a very healthy food.

Below, the Jonagold is a cross between a Jonathan and a Golden Delicious apple

APPLE

Apple blossoms cluster together in groups of five. The largest blossom in the center of the five-flower cluster is called the king.

Above, a pruned tree
Right, unpicked apples
Far right, apple trees in full bloom

The apple tree itself is useful, too. Homeowners plant it for the beauty and aroma of its spring blossoms, and wild birds, squirrels, mice, rabbits, bears, and deer enjoy its fruit. An apple tree's wood can be used for fuel, made into furniture, or carved by hobbyists.

The apple has been an important part of people's lives for millions of years. Today's apple growers are producing more apples than ever, and people are buying them. It's easy to appreciate what a unique and versatile fruit the apple has become.

Glossary

Doctors use an **anesthetic** to numb a patient's sense of pain.

An **antiseptic** is a substance that kills germs.

Apple **cider** is a drink made from pressed apples.

Commercial growing operations are businesses whose focus is growing and shipping a large quantity of apples.

A tree that is **cultivated** has been planted and cared for by people who will gather its fruit.

When a tree is **dormant**, it is alive but not growing.

Grafting is the process of taking a branch or bud from one tree and joining it to another tree, where it continues to grow.

To gather a ripe apple is to **harvest** it.

Orchards are areas of land where fruit trees are grown.

Pollen is the sticky, yellow powder in the center of flowers.

Pomology is the study of apple growing.

When growers **prune** a tree, they trim or cut its branches.

Rootstock is the part of the tree onto which the scion is grafted and continues to grow.

A **waxed** apple is one that has a light coating of harmless chemicals that keeps the apple from shriveling.

Index